DOROTHY ROBINSON

DOT'ISMS and INSPIRATIONAL POEMS

HOV
PUBLISHING

DOT'ISMS & INSPIRATIONAL POEMS

HOV Publishing is a division of HOV, LLC.
www.hovpub.com
www.90daybookcreation.com
hopeofvision@gmail.com

Front Cover and inside Illustration by Dorothy Robinson
Inside layout by Hope of Vision Designs
Editor/Proofread: HOV Publishing Editorial Team

Contact the Author at robinsonc753@gmail.com

For further information regarding special discounts on bulk purchases, please email robinsonc753@gmail.com.

ISBN Paperback: 978-1-955107-47-1

ISBN eBook: 978-1-955107-46-4

Printed in the United States of America

ACKNOWLEDGEMENTS

To Virginia Menskey for starting the typing process for the book.

To my daughter Candi, for typing, preliminary editing, transferring info to the publisher, and overall support through this process.

To Rev. Robert Jackson, Jr. for his support in promoting the book.

To Lori McDonald for suggesting the name of the book.

To Judy Owens, who I can't thank enough for introducing me to Germaine Miller-Summers, CEO of HOV Publishing. This is my first book and Germaine has been wonderful, taking me step by step through the publishing process.

And to all those who encouraged me to publish my book.

Thank you.

CONTENTS

DOT'ISMS

IMAGE ILLUSTRATED BY DOROTHY ROBINSON

DOT'ISM #1

Christians should not be afraid of being robed or receiving bodily harm from criminals.
The worry should be; if something happens to me this minute, will I go to heaven.

DOT'ISM #2

God does not put sickness on us. When we sin, He allows sickness to happen.

DOT'ISM #3

If God is good all the time, how can he do evil to you?

DOT'ISM #4

Two things God gave man that is harming the world: choice and sex.

DOT'ISM #5

Satan can give you great material riches, but he has no place to take you but hell.

DOT'ISM #6

Some people blame God for bad things that happen to them. They say that God predestined their lives. God does not predestine lives. You predestine your life by the choices you make.

DOT'ISM #7

God is fair. He even gave his angels a choice. That is why Lucifer had to be kicked out of heaven.

DOT'ISM #8

The writer of the song "Lord Please Don't move the Mountain, buy give me the strength to climb" really understood Jesus' parable of the mustard seed. If you have faith of a mustard seed and say to that mountain move, it will move.

DOT'ISM #9

Some people read and study the Bible with a closed mind. They see what the Bible says, but they don't see what the Bible is saying. (In all thy getting, get understanding)

DOT'ISM #10

God kept his promise. He promised the people of Israel a king when they asked for one. He gave them king after king. Most of them did evil. Then God gave them a real king, Jesus.

DOT'ISM #11

Some people are loving their children to Hell, by giving them everything they want and letting them have their way with everything. (Spare the discipline, spoil the child).

DOT'ISM #12

There are three kinds of people:
(1) people who do right because it
is right to do right, (2) people who
do right because they are guided
to do right, (3) people who have to
be punished to do right.

DOT'ISM #13

You are not what you used to be.
Tomorrow you will not be what you
are today. You grow from the past
to the future.

DOT'ISM #14

Don't study the Bible just to know the Bible. Study the Bible to do the Bible.

DOT'ISM #15

Children need to be taught threefold, (1) Spiritual, (2) Academic, (3) Economic.

DOT'ISM #16

Are you who you were created to be or are you who you were taught to be?

DOT'ISM #17

Never stop learning. Trust in God as you are learning, and learning becomes wisdom.

DOT'ISM #18

God will get you through anything, but you have to have the will to go through.

DOT'ISM #19

When you put your trust fully in man, you are really putting your trust in Satan.

DOT'ISM #20

Some people blame God to much for things that happen to them. They give Satan to much credit for things that happen to them. They fail to take the blame for the bad choices they make.

DOT'ISM #21

Wearing your best clothes to church is a symbol like baptism. You are giving God your best. Going to church as you are is a symbol of giving God what you have.

DOT'ISM #22

Jesus took the blame for our sins and took them from the cross to hell. Our sins were so many that it took Him three days to leave them in Hell. Jesus took them to Hell because Hell is the only place for sin. Jesus had to take our sins to Hell because they couldn't go the heaven with Him.

DOT'ISM #23

There are Christians, and there are saved Christians.

DOT'ISM #24

When you eat non-nourishing food, the stomach is happy, but the body suffers for need of nourishing food.

DOT'ISM #25

People go to God in different ways. Some on their knees as the woman with an issue of blood, and some from treetops as did Nicodemus. It does not matter how you go to God.
What matters is that you go.

DOT'ISM #26

Don't stop going to church because of church devils (hypocrites). That is why they are there, to stop you from going.

DOT'ISM #27

Bad circumstances are lessened, while you are hoping.

DOT'ISM #28

Many people today refuse to see or admit their wrongness.

DOT'ISM #29

The first computer was made by God...man's brain.

DOT'ISM #30

Don't look at a task and say, "I can't". Look at it and say, "I'll try."

DOT'ISM #31

Young people stay away from church because of adult hypocrites.

DOT'ISM #32

It is what it is, but it does not have to stay what it is. Everything can be improved.

DOT'ISM #33

When the world makes your life sour, sweeten it by adding God.

DOT'ISM #34

You can keep the Sabbath holy, even if you have to work. Make your customers happy.

DOT'ISM #35

Children do what their parents do, and what their parents don't tell them not to do.

DOT'ISM #36

Your choices determine the type of life you live. Your choices also affect the lives of others.

DOT'ISM #37

People's needs are not always met with money. Sometimes a beautiful spirit and a loving smile will do.

DOT'ISM #38

Patience and hope will take you a long way.

DOT'ISM #39

Positive attitude: positive life. Negative attitude: negative life. Keep a positive attitude in the worst of times and you will win.

DOT'ISM #40

Don't get so busy that you leave God out. Let your business be a relationship with Him.

DOT'ISM #41

Have courage and faith to face any problems you may have.

DOT'ISM #42

Me and God together can do anything.

DOT'ISM #43

For a brighter future you must accept the past, trust God to handle the future, and make the most of the time He has given you today.

DOT'ISM #44

Plan your goals and to-do-list, but let God direct you through them.

DOT'ISM #45

God wants you to plan ahead, but He wants you to plan in His name, then your plans will come to fruition.

DOT'ISM #46

Do something positive every day because God has given it to you.

DOT'ISM #47

The great commission Jesus gave us was to spread the Gospel to all the world. Christians who are not ordained preachers can spread the Gospel by: (1) being a good example; (2) teaching; (3) having the courage to speak up when they see injustice; (4) being quick to forgive; (5) seeing some good in everyone; (6) understanding God's word before passing it on; (7) loving people to the point that you understand their wrongdoing.

DOT'ISM #48

Why envy anything others have when God's grace and eternal life is greater than anything others can have.

DOT'ISM #49

Character is what you are behind closed doors.

DOT'ISM #50

Be a best friend to somebody, as Jesus is a best friend to you.

DOT'ISM #51

When Satan throws you a curve, throw a prayer at him.

DOT'ISM #52

You should not hesitate to forgive others because God does not hesitate to forgive you.

DOT'ISM #53

God's gift of a supply of the Holy Spirit, is better that a supply of money.

DOT'ISM #54

Negative people will rob you of
your courage.

DOT'ISM #55

A good friend is more concerned
about what is best for you rather
than being accepted by you.

DOT'ISM #56

When we are young, we spend our
health on wealth. When we get old,
we spend our wealth to get health.

DOT'ISM #57

All decisions have consequences.

DOT'ISM #58

Generosity is more that giving things, it is also giving freely of Christ's love.

DOT'ISM #59

God produces miracles every day, raising the sun, raising you, etc.

DOT'ISM #60

Don't be a workaholic. God cannot use a tired soul.

DOT'ISM #61

A smile will break up a frown.

DOT'ISM #62

Make your thought and attitude Christ like to better yourself.

DOT'ISM #63

Worry not, and you will have more strength to fight your problems.

DOT'ISM #64

Knowing and doing God's word will keep you from temptations.

DOT'ISM #65

God is always on stand-by, just plug Him in when you need Him.

DOT'ISM #66

Let God guide your daily activities
and you will avoid trouble.

DOT'ISM #67

Frustration makes a problem
worst, calm down.

DOT'ISM #68

Forgive, no matter how big
the hurt.

DOT'ISM #69

Envy knocks contentment out the door.

DOT'ISM #70

You cannot sleep. You cannot wake up. You cannot walk. You cannot see. You cannot hear. You cannot do anything without God's help.

DOT'ISM #71

Look hard enough and you may find good in that bad person.

DOT'ISM #72

Fear takes away faith and trust
in God.

DOT'ISM #73

Repent by actions and not just
by words.

DOT'ISM #74

Patience pays, impatience costs.

DOT'ISM #75

With God on your side, no problem can keep you down.

DOT'ISM #76

When your friend is down, don't show pity, show courage.

DOT'ISM #77

Let your eyes see what is true.
Let your ears hear what is true.
Let your mind think what is true.
Let your mouth speak what is true.

DOT'ISM #78

What you are and what you may become depends on the choices you make.

DOT'ISM #79

God made you. Jesus saved you. So please only them.

DOT'ISM #80

Faith builds courage.

DOT'ISM #81

It is better to be great in God's eyes by being meek and humble, than being great in man's eyes by being worldly successful.

DOT'ISM #82

Do not allow your past to rob you of your future.

DOT'ISM #83

Give God some silent time each day.

DOT'ISM #84

Righteous indignation is OK, but angry spoken words that hurt are not OK.

DOT'ISM #85

What you think feeds your soul, so let the words of your mouth and the meditations of your heart be pleasing to God.

DOT'ISM #86

Be cheerful for others, even if you have reasons to be sad.

DOT'ISM #87

The more faith you have the bigger
the problems you can solve.

DOT'ISM #88

God's way will get you farther than
your way will.

DOT'ISM #89

If you put too much trust in your
friends, they can lead you to stray.

DOT'ISM #90

It is impossible to have a perfect physical life. Prepare for that perfect eternal life.

DOT'ISM #91

Listen more, speak less.

DOT'ISM #92

A good mentor will hold people accountable for their actions.

DOT'ISM #93

When you put yourself first, you put God on the back burner.

DOT'ISM #94

Unforgiveness is an everlasting sin.

DOT'ISM #95

Don't think of a spanking from God as punishment, think of it as a test. Just think of the joy when you make it through the test.

DOT'ISM #96

Grumpy Christians please no one but Satan.

DOT'ISM #97

You may be doing alright, but with a relationship with God, you will do better.

DOT'ISM #98

Pray with patience.

DOT'ISM #99

Hope keeps dreams alive and
makes them come true.

DOT'ISM #100

The greatest blessings are given to
you when you give kindness to
others.

DOT'ISM #101

Don't blame, think of ways to
fix it.

DOT'ISM #102

Your decisions can make or break you.

DOT'ISM #103

Your body is God's temple, when you abuse it, you abuse God.

DOT'ISM #104

If what you hoped for never came through, at least you never had a bad moment doubting it.

DOT'ISM #105

Laughter heals.

DOT'ISM #106

For all that you accomplish, the glory does not belong to you, it belongs to God who enabled you.

DOT'ISM #107

To follow you must stay behind. To lead you must stay in front.

DOT'ISM #108

Faith only works with work.

DOT'ISM #109

A loving family and true friends are

two of God's greatest gifts.

DOT'ISM #110

When we are born again,

we never die.

DOT'ISM #111

Commitment builds good

character.

DOT'ISM #112

Good pressure is a strong desire to follow God's will. Bad pressure is a strong desire to keep up with the world.

DOT'ISM #113

Trust God and fear will jump out the window.

DOT'ISM #114

It is stupid not to forgive, because it helps the forgiver more that it helps the forgiven.

DOT'ISM #115

When bad things happen to you, put hope ahead of them and watch God wash them away.

DOT'ISM #116

Giving is more blessed that receiving because you are blessed to have it to give.

DOT'ISM #117

Don't hog-up all of God's blessings for yourself, share them.

DOT'ISM #118

If you wear God's armor you will not need pepper spray, guns, or knives to protect yourself.

DOT'ISM #119

Responsibilities come whether you take them or not.

DOT'ISM #120

When you see the good in others it makes the goodness come out in you.

DOT'ISM #121

Don't just talk the talk. Do the talk.

DOT'ISM #122

Don't let age keep you from being enthusiastic about life.

DOT'ISM #123

Live within your means. Save money from every paycheck. Never spend more than you make.

DOT'ISM #124

If you know a person who is too bad and mean to love, you can love the meanness and badness out of them. Love conquers all.

DOT'ISM #125

Words can help or hurt. Be careful what you say.

DOT'ISM #126

Walk with wise people and become wise.

DOT'ISM #127

Anger leads to unforgiveness. Unforgiveness leads to discontentment. Discontentment leads to spiritual death.

DOT'ISM #128

God is Mr. Fix it. Give Him a try.

DOT'ISM #129

Live life with a smile and hopefulness, which shows godliness.

DOT'ISM #130

Knowledge is knowing man's world. Wisdom is knowing where man's world belongs.

DOT'ISM #131

God's strength does not get tired.

DOT'ISM #132

There are only two things we have to do in life, we have to die, and we have to live until we die. The rest is made up.

DOT'ISM #133

Exercise alone will not get you fit.
You need God in the mix.

DOT'ISM #134

God gave you, you. Why not give
Him a little time each day?

DOT'ISM #135

Bad habits, troubled life. Good
habits, peaceful life.

DOT'ISM #136

Curiosity is helpful, it helps you learn more about things.

DOT'ISM #137

Rely on self, you will fail. Rely on man, you will fail. Rely on God, you will succeed.

DOT'ISM #138

God gives us something to be joyful about every time we get out of bed...the day.

DOT'ISM #139

A wee bit of doubt will kill faith.

DOT'ISM #140

If you think no evil, speak no evil,

do no evil, then good character will

form with good works.

DOT'ISM #141

Tell the truth even if it hurts.

DOT'ISM #142

Love is a greater gift than silver

and gold.

DOT'ISM #143

Don't use failure as an excuse for a pity party. Learn what needs to be done and do it and keep stepping upward.

DOT'ISM #144

Hope will get you through this life with only a few scars.

DOT'ISM #145

Hatred is a path to hell. Forgiving is the path to heaven.

DOT'ISM #146

Speak encouraging words to everyone.

DOT'ISM #147

What you decide today may come back to haunt you tomorrow. Include God when making decisions.

DOT'ISM #148

God does his best work through your faith.

DOT'ISM #149

Families will not be together forever; therefore we should love and nourish each other while we are together.

DOT'ISM #150

A true friend understands that a correction is not a criticism.

DOT'ISM #151

Show love and kindness rather than clothes and hair dos.

DOT'ISM #152

Your tone of voice can change the meaning of your words.

DOT'ISM #153

Plan for the worst but look for the best.

DOT'ISM #154

When you start going all the time, you need to ask yourself: What am I running from?

DOT'ISM #155

Can Not is not in God's
vocabulary.

DOT'ISM #156

Boast about me to my back, but
criticize me to my face, so I can do
better.

DOT'ISM #157

Knowledge is taught by man;
wisdom is given by God.

DOT'ISM #158

Some Christians have a relationship with God as parent. Some Christians have a relationship with God as friend, like Moses had with Him.

DOT'ISM #159

Wisdom is solid, knowledge is fleeting.

DOT'ISM #160

God saves me a lot of trips to the doctor.

DOT'ISM #161

There are somethings we can do
with God's help, and there are
other things only God can do.

DOT'ISM #162

We fear the first death (physical).
The second death (spiritual) is the
one we should fear.

DOT'ISM #163

The healthier you keep your body,
the better you can serve God.

DOT'ISM #164

It is easier to say what we believe,

than to do what we believe.

DOT'ISM #165

Good leaders are scarce, so I am

following myself.

DOT'ISM #166

Whatever you assume to be true,

will become real to you.

DOT'ISM #167

You really don't believe it if you don't live it.

DOT'ISM #168

The more investment you have in your beliefs, the harder it is to change them.

DOT'ISM #169

The family was the first governing unit.

DOT'ISM #170

God does not promise immediate success, but He does promise to help us find a way to achieve. But we must practice the Fruit of the Spirit (love, patience, joy, faith, peace, kindness, goodness, gentleness, and self-control).

DOT'ISM #171

It takes stable families to build stable nations, churches, and schools.

DOT'ISM #172

When God blesses one old person fruitfully, a lot of persons get blessed because that is one old person they will not have to worry about.

DOT'ISM #173

Nothing can be made or done without God. God made man who makes the things; God created the things that man used to make things.

DOT'ISM #174

God is truly everywhere if you look
for him.

DOT'ISM #175

Loving is like forgiving:

You love just because
You forgive just because

DOT'ISM #176

You are never too old to be born
again.

DOT'ISM #177

Write your daily thoughts down,

they will do you good.

DOT'ISM #178

Some things you bought cheap

years ago, are treasures today.

DOT'ISM #179

God has a reason for everything

he does.

DOT'ISM #180

It is what it is, but it does not have to be what it is if you do something about it.

DOT'ISM #181

God is merciful, He gives fresh air to the murderer, the drug dealer, and the crooked politicians, just as he gives to Christians.

DOT'ISM #182

Never discipline your child when you are angry, it turns to abuse.

DOT'ISM #183

To help save the environment, recycle all paper goods, except tissue.

DOT'ISM #184

Some people will never allow themselves to think. They just go through life believing what others say and doing what others do.

DOT'ISM #185

God did not give me 96 years to sit down and do nothing.

DOT'ISM #186

When we were simple people, we enjoyed simple pleasures. Now that we have become sophisticated, nothing pleases us.

DOT'ISM #187

Things work better when you add common sense to what you learn in books.

DOT'ISM #188

Don't let education lead you to Hell!

DOT'ISM #189

Don't let the dislike of a person's way lead you to hate the person!

DOT'ISM #190

Don't give the battle to Satan, make him work for it and loose through your faith in God.

DOT'ISM #191

Much of what happens to you when you get older depends on what you did when you were young.

DOT'ISM #192

If the book's A doesn't work, you will need common sense to work B.

DOT'ISM #193

Ask for help if you need it.

DOT'ISM #194

When you start to think of what you don't have, check out what you do have, and you will realize that you have more than what you don't have.

DOT'ISM #195

Forgive yourself for your past sins and God will forgive you for your future sins.

DOT'ISM #196

Some people try to beat the devil out of their children, rather to love and explain the devil out of them.

DOT'ISM #197

Your mood gives you a facial expression, and your facial expression tells your mood.

DOT'ISM #198

Don't blame me for not keeping in touch. Blame my couch. Every time I sit on it, it puts me to sleep.

DOT'ISM #199

It is ok to start good trouble. America needs a lot of it.

DOT'ISM #200

God did not give us the Bible just to read it. He gave us the Bible to believe it.

DOT'ISM #201

It is better to miss a deal, than to fall for a scam.

DOT'ISM #202

Some churches have become so modern that they have modernized Jesus and God out.

INSPIRATIONAL POEMS

IMAGE ILLUSTRATED BY DOROTHY ROBINSON

A MESSAGE TO ALL TEENAGERS

"What's The Purpose"

I was wondering why the white police were killing so many black men. I am still wondering.

Teenagers, you seem to be living in a vacuum of false thoughts that this life is everything.

That when you die that is the end of everything.

Teen have you ever heard of life after death, or eternal life?

When Jesus died on the cross, he gave everybody (the good and bad) eternal life or life after death.

People who did good in this life will have a happy eternal life. People who

did bad in this life will burn in Hell
forever with no relief.

You still don't believe?
Look at it this way.

If you die believing in life after death
and find out that there is no life after
death, you will have lost nothing.

If you die disbelieving in life after death
and find out that there is life after death,
you will have lost everything and end up
in the burning pit.

Which choice will you choose?

~ Dorothy Alexander Robinson

A MINUTE TESTAMENT

One day while on the job vacuuming, the thought…**you are a strong black woman** came to me. I was 76 at the time and all my friends had retired, so at lunch I wrote this poem.

I am *a strong black woman*,
And I know it.
I was born premature,
But I survived on my mother's milk and my family's love.

I am *a strong black woman*,
And I know it.
I survived the great depression.
When sometimes all we had to eat was wild greens and wild meat.

I am *a strong black woman,*
And I know it.
I lived in segregation and came through it not hating the white man.

I am *a strong black woman,*
And I know it.
My mother died when I was nine.
At fourteen I had to help my papa keep
house for three younger siblings.
Still, I managed to finish high school
and three years of college.

I am *a strong black woman,*
And I know it.
I was married forty-three years and
raised a daughter to love God
and respect herself and others.

Why am I a strong black woman?
Because my parents and my village
taught me to love God, respect myself
and others.

I AM A STRONG BLACK WOMAN
And I Know It.

~ Dorothy Alexander Robinson

COMFORTABLE

One night after bible study, we were discussing
why more people don't come to bible study.
They are in their comfort zone and don't want to
come out.

If you learn better, you will have to do better.
This is why the poem came to me.

Pam had a large family with
large problems.
Pam's friend told her to come to Bible
class, and she may find answers to her
problems.

Says Pam:
I do not wish to be informed.
I may have to reform.
I am comfortable where I am.
Thank you, mam.

Pam got lucky and hit the numbers for
$100,000.
Her friend told her to go to the
community center and learn how to
invest money.

Says Pam:
I do not wish to be informed.
I may have to reform.
I am comfortable where I am.
Thank you, mam.
Six months later Pam was broke and
did not have a job.
Pam's friend told her to come to the
town hall, and she would show her how
to apply for welfare.

Says Pam:
I do not wish to be informed.
I may have to reform.
I am comfortable where I am.
Thank you, mam.

An unexplainable lump grew on Pam's
hand.
Her friend told her to come with her to
the doctor and he would diagnose the
lump.

Says Pam:
I do not wish to be informed.
I may have to reform.
I am comfortable where I am.
Thank you, mam.

Pam died from the lump which was
curable.
What did her friend put on her
tombstone?

Pam did not wish to be informed.
She would have had to reform.
She is comfortable where she is.
Thank you, mam.

~ Dorothy Alexander Robinson

CONFESSION

If God would give me a complete make-over, I would ask him to tear down the times that I put him on the back burner so that I could have a good time.

If God would give me a complete make-over, I would ask him to tear down the times that I hurt someone through actions or words.

If God would give me a complete make-over, I would ask him to tear down the times that I fought with my playmates.

If God would give me a complete make-over, I would ask him to tear down the times that I thought it was not necessary to attend church.

If God would give me a complete
make-over, I would ask him to tear
down the time that I lost faith in him
and left college.

If God would give me a complete
make-over, I would ask him to fill me
with the Holy Spirit so that I could resist
Satan minute by minute, hour by hour,
day by day, month by month and year
by year.

~ Dorothy Alexander Robinson

I WANT

I want a blessing of good health.

I want a blessing of a fine mansion.

I want a blessing of a fabulous car.

I want a blessing of designer clothes.

I want a blessing of expensive jewelry.

I want a blessing of a big bank account.

I want a blessing of a large yacht.

I want, I want, I want…

But most of all Lord, I want to know and understand your Word.

~ Dorothy Alexander Robinson

IT WAS NECESSARY

The Women's Day theme for 2023 at Bethel AME Church inspired me to write this poem.

God put Adam and Eve out of the Garden of Eden because they listened to Satan and ate from one of the trees that God forbade them to eat from.

It was necessary because if they had eaten from the tree of life, evil would have lived forever.

For God makes all things good for those who love him.

Cain killed his brother Abel because God accepted Abel's offer picked from the trees and refused Cain's offering picked up from the ground.

It was necessary for God to show us that He wanted our best, not our left-over time, talent, and money.

For God makes all things good for those who love him.

God caused the whole earth to flood and killed all humankind except one family. All other humankind had become totally corrupt.

It was necessary so God could bring up a generation fit for his son Jesus to be born in.

For God makes all things good for those that love him.

God killed all of Pharaoh's first born because he refused to let the people of Israel leave with Moses.

It was necessary so that the people of Israel could possess the land promised.

For God makes all things good for those who love him.

Soon after the Israelites left with Moses, Pharaoh changed his mind and he and his army followed them to bring them back to Egypt. The Israelites had reached the Red Sea with Pharaoh close behind them. Now they are caught between the devil and the deep Red Sea.

God divided the sea so the Israelites could cross it.

When the Israelites were safely over, Pharaoh's army entered the open sea. God closed the sea and all of Pharaoh's army drowned.

It was necessary so that God could show us that He can and will do the impossible and let Pharaoh know that He, God is always in charge.

For God makes all things good for those who love him.

God sanctified his son Jesus to be
crucified on the cross.

It was necessary so that everybody
could have grace and be forgiven over
and over.

*For God makes all things good for those
who love him.*

After three days God raised Jesus from
the dead. Jesus walked and talked to
his disciples and many other people
before he ascended to heaven.

It was necessary to give us life after
physical death.

*For God made all things good for those
who love him.*

~ Dorothy Alexander Robinson

MY TONGUE

I was inspired to write this poem after I heard a visiting preacher preach about the damage the tongue can do to one's spiritual life.

August 12, 2019

My mind keeps my tongue busy every awake hour.

It causes my tongue to speak wasteful words.

It causes my tongue to speak hurtful words.

It causes my tongue to speak meaningless words.

It causes my tongue to speak dying words.

But when I put my mind on Jesus, my tongue became a different organ.

I speak words of encouragement.

I speak words of kindness.

I speak words of joy.

I speak words of peace.

Oh, what a joy to have a different wag
of the tongue!!!

~ Dorothy Alexander Robinson

On Earth

On earth,
I do not wish for a fabulous house.
I just want a convenient house.

On earth,
I do not wish for the most luxurious car.
I just want a comfortable car.

On earth,
I do not wish to have the latest fashions.
I just want a decent change of clothes.

On earth,
I do not wish for the most
expensive food.
I just want good nourishing food.

On earth,
I do not wish for a body like
Wonder Woman.
I just want a body that is healthy enough
to do God's work.

But when I get to heaven
I want everything that God has
promised.

With that everlasting body,
I am going to walk all over New
Jerusalem on those streets of gold.

I am going to invite some saints
to dinner,
With expensive food in a fabulous
house that never needs repair.

After dinner I am going to sleep in the
most comfortable and luxurious bed
like sleeping on a cloud.

The next morning, I am going to Jesus
and ask him to let me go to the Father.
To see Him face to face and thank Him
for everything from earth to heaven.
Amen.

~ Dorothy Alexander Robinson

ONE TEAR

**A.K.A. mom, momma, shorty,
granny, so grown.**
February 18, 2021

Do not mourn for me when I'm gone.
Think of my…
Delicious potato salad
Tasty fruit cake
Out of this world Pear Preserves and
Refreshing Wisbar punch

Cry one tear

Do not mourn for me when I'm gone.
Long before this thing happened to me,
I made peace with God.
Followed His commandments.
When I messed up, I repented.

Cry one tear

Remember the happy times we had together.
Now go and live the rest of your life for God.

Be Happy
            Cry one tear

~ Dorothy Alexander Robinson

SELF MADE

God, you made us so self-sufficient that
we don't need you.
We think we are everything and a bag
of potato chips.

God, you made us so self-sufficient that
we don't need your sunlight.
We took the river that you created,
dammed it up and made our own light.
When you take your sun down, we turn
on our own light.

God, you made us so self-sufficient that
we don't have to depend on your legs to
transport us.
We made cars, trains, ships and planes
to transport us and fast!

*God, you made us so self-sufficient that
we don't have to wait for you to hew
down the trees or dry up the river.*

We chain saw the trees down and
move the river.

*God, you made us so self-sufficient that
we don't need to use your creation of
the mouth to communicate.*

We invented the smart phone so we
can communicate by texting without
opening our mouth.

*God, you made us so self-sufficient that
we don't have to wait for you to change
seasons to be comfortable.*

We invented the furnace to keep
warm in the winter, and the air
conditioner to keep cool in the
summer.

We have warmth in your cold season
and cool in your hot season.

*God, you made us so self-sufficient that
we are too ignorant to realize that it is
you who made us.*

> That it is you who created the
> minerals and the tools to make these
> things.

> That it is you who gave us the brains
> to make these things.

*God, forgive our self-sufficient selves.
For we know not what we do.*

> We know not that all you have to do
> is cause a great earthquake or a
> mighty storm and everything ends.

God forgive our self-sufficient selves!!

~ Dorothy Alexander Robinson

SPECIAL

The inspiration for this poem came while watching a TV show where the females portrayed low self-esteem.

August 12, 2019

I walk around with my head held high.
Some people look at me and say,
She thinks she's cute, maybe so.
But I am special.

When God made the earth, he spoke
everything into being.

Water and land separate!!
Up sprang mountains, hills, valleys, and
plateaus.
In rolled oceans, rivers, and lakes.

Creatures of the sea come forward!!
In swam sea creatures of all kinds,
Whales, dolphins, eels, and porgies.

Plants come forward!!
Up sprang plants of all kinds,

Tall trees, bushes, vines, and edible
plants.

Fowls of the air come forward!!
Away in the air flew fowls of all kinds,
Mighty eagles, hawks, pigeons, and
sparrows.

Four-legged beast come forward!!
In ran animals of all kinds,
Lions, tigers, bears, cats, and dogs.

But when it came to me!!
He T O U C H E D me.
With his mighty hands he scooped
up some clay,
And molded this beautiful body.

And if that wasn't enough,
He resuscitated me with his own breath,
And made me a living soul.

That is why I am special!!!
And so are you, and you, and you.

~ Dorothy Alexander Robinson

UNEXPECTED VISIT

"Date Written"

December 17, 2016

Jesus came by to visit me the other day,
And I was not ready for his visit.

I heard a knock on the door and
thought to myself,
Now who could that be for I am NOT
expecting anyone today.

I went to the door and called out
WHO IS IT.
I heard a voice say,
It is me, Jesus.
I came to visit with you today.

I opened the door and said, Jesus can
you come back another day.
My house is not clean. I was just about
to dust my bible off and start reading it.

Jesus said, Dust that bible, read that
bible, get that bible in your heart.
I am coming again, and you may not
have time to dust your bible,
so, prepare yourself now for my
second coming.

~ Dorothy Alexander Robinson

WALKING IN GOD

God, it must have been a sad day for you,
When your only companions
"Adam and Eve"
Had to hide from you because of what they
had done against you.

God, it must have been a sad day for you,
When you had to destroy by water your
favorite creation, "man."

God, it must have been a sad day for you,
When you had to make the utmost sacrifice
By giving your only son to again, save your
favorite creation, "man."

God, thank you for loving me so much
that you did sacrifice your only son.
Now your favorite creation "man" has
chance after chance to get it right.

~ Dorothy Alexander Robinson

WHAT'S THE PURPOSE

---

*I was wondering why the white police were killing
so many black men. I am still wondering.*

What's The Purpose…
  A white policeman beating a black woman.
  He calls it carrying out the law.
  If any other man was beating a woman
  for any reason,
  It would be called domestic brutality.

What's The Purpose…
  A white policeman choking a black man
  to death.
  He calls it carrying out the law.
  If any other person chocked a man to
  Death,
  It would be called murder.

What's The Purpose…
  A white policeman shoots a black
  teenager with his hands in the air six times.
  He calls it protecting his life from the teen.
  If anyone else shot a person six times,
  It would be called murder.

What's The Purpose…
Was it to keep law and order?
Was it for the policemen to get their
anger off?
Was it for the policemen to get their
hate of blacks off?

What's The Purpose…
Is it that politicians are not doing their job?
Is it that the churches are not doing their
job?
Is it that families are not doing their job?
Is it that black people are not voting
enough?

What's The Purpose…
Is God saying I am turning my face
from you?
Is God saying that it's the lack of
knowledge of him?
Is God saying come back to me or die?
Is God saying we have strayed so far
from him?

What's The Purpose…
  So, to everything there is a purpose.
  So come on church,
  Come on politicians,
  Come on family,
  Come on black voters,

Find the purpose and let's stop this
madness.

What's the purpose…

> ~ Dorothy Alexander Robinson

WHERE DID THE TIME GO

When I was young time didn't matter
    I could do a day's work.
    I could cook.
    I could clean.
    I could do laundry.
    I could iron.
    I could care for my child.
    I could teach church school.
    I could go to church meetings.
    I could go to community meetings.
     all in one week

It's still 24 hours in a day.

Now I cook.
    I take a nap.
    I dust one room.
    I take a nap.
    I do laundry.
    I take a nap.

That is where time goes,
It flies while I am sleep.

~ Dorothy Alexander Robinson

THE ALTAR

One Sunday I went to church all prayed up and ready to worship. When it came time for the preached word, the pastor seemed to be struggling to get his sermon going. I looked away from him and looked at the altar to pray that he gets it together. Instead of a prayer coming to me, this poem came to me, and I wrote it then and there on the church bulletin.

Don't ask me if the pastor ever got his sermon together because I was busy writing.

August 12, 2019

In my church there is a very special place to me.

The middle of the altar.

Where as a baby, my parents gave me to God.

In the middle of the altar.

Where at the proper age I gave myself to God.

In the middle of the altar.

Where I married the love of my life.

In the middle of the altar.

Where we gave our offspring to God.

In the middle of the altar.

Where I will begin my eternal life
with God.

Amen, Amen, Amen

~ Dorothy Alexander Robinson

IMAGINATION

Sometimes my imagination runs away with me.

I imagine that God, Jesus, and Satan are talking to me.

I wake up in the morning and thank God for waking me up.

Asking Him for his energy, strength, guidance, and wisdom.

Out of the bed I go, use the bathroom, lean on the sink, and begin to brush my teeth.

I hear God say, that is not my strength, it's yours. I straighten up and finish brushing my teeth.

After breakfast I begin to plan the chores for the day.

I hear Satan say, you need to rest today.

So off to the couch I go and lie down. A few minutes pass, then I hear God say, you asked for my strength so get up and use it.

I get up and begin my chores. The chores are finished sooner than I planned.

So, I am walking around in the house saying thank you Jesus, thank you, thank you, thank you Jesus, thank you, thank you.

I hear Jesus say, "Now What."

I answer Jesus and say, I was just thanking you for all the things you have done for my 98 years, all you are doing for me now, and all that you are going to do.

Jesus says alright daughter, I hear you so keep on thanking me.

To Satan I say, did you hear that.

You stay away from me Satan because I believe that my imagination will STEP me through those pearly gates into that golden city.

Thank you, Jesus. Thank you, God.

~ Dorothy Alexander Robinson

ABOUT THE AUTHOR

I grew up with an inferiority complex. I was born in the coalfields of Benhem, Kentucky and raised in the coalfields of Stonega, Virginia. City people looked down on farmers and coalfield people.

After I finished high school, I would go to Massachusetts each summer to make money for college.

Except for the first summer, I stayed almost two years, doing domestic work for six months and working at the Boston Navy Yard doing defense work for over a year.

I applied too late to get into Virginia State College, so I ended up going to Bluefield State College located in Bluefield West Virginia.

After having to leave school in the first semester of my fourth year due to lack of funds, I migrated to Connecticut in 1947. In 1950 I went back to Virginia, married, and my husband and I came to Connecticut.

In 1968 I began to teach Church School and started seriously studying the bible. I learned that there are no superior or inferior people. Material possessions doesn't make you superior, nor does the lack of material possessions make you inferior.

Soon after, I became the Church School Superintendent, Director of Commission on Christian Education, a Trustee, and a Director on the Board of Directors of Friendship House. All this at the same time.

Now at the age of 98, I am publishing my first book that I wrote after my 91st birthday.

MS. DOROTHY ROBINSON

DOT'ISMS *and* INSPIRATIONAL POEMS